SPENCER TRACY

A Life from Beginning to End

Copyright © 2022 by Hourly History.

Table of Contents

Introduction

Spencer Tracy, the man who would launch himself into the stratosphere of Hollywood superstardom, began life in Milwaukee, Wisconsin, on April 5, 1900. He was the son of truck salesman John Edward Tracy and his wife, Caroline. Spencer's father was an Irish Catholic, and his mother a Protestant. It was his father's religious ways that apparently won out since Spencer would ultimately be raised a Catholic and attend Catholic schools.

At around 15 years of age, Spencer was in attendance at Milwaukee's St. John's Cathedral School for boys. His family then made their way to Kansas City, Missouri, where Spencer was placed in a boarding school called St. Mary's. Both being away from his family and being away from the hustle and bustle of city life—and especially the old Milwaukee movie house he had enjoyed frequently as a boy—were an adjustment for him. The adjustment would be a temporary one, however, since his father John's job fell through, and in less than a year, the Tracys were back in Milwaukee.

It was shortly after Spencer's return that he decided to drop out of school so that he could join up with the Navy in 1917. World War I was in full force at this time, and Spencer, now 18 years old, wanted to do his part. He did not end up serving overseas, however, since he was still in training by the time the war ended in 1918. After the war, he received an honorable discharge.

Upon Spencer's return home, he went back to school, where he managed to finish up the last few classes he needed in order to get his high school diploma. He then used his diploma, plus credit acquired from his time in the Navy, to go to college. In the spring of 1921, Spencer was enrolled at Ripon College, located some 90 miles to the north of Milwaukee.

Tracy threw himself headlong into his studies. Initially, he decided to major in medicine, but after he made his way to the stage in a school theatrical production of *The Truth*, Spencer Tracy suddenly knew what his major life's work would be.

Chapter One

Acting at College

"I'm disappointed in acting as a craft. I want everything to go back to Orson Welles and fake noses and changing your voice. It's become so much about personality."

—Spencer Tracy

In 1921, Spencer Tracy was thrilled to star in a leading role for a theatrical production of *The Truth* at Ripon College. Spencer played the part of Tom Warder, a man coming to grips with a marriage coming undone from intrigue and deceit. Spencer studied his lines well and made sure to capture the raw emotion of the troubled character that he played.

It was on June 21, 1921, at Rippon Municipal Auditorium that Spencer Tracy first took the stage. The character that Spencer portrayed emerged in the opening scenes as a straightforward and trusting husband, hanging on every word of his scheming wife, Becky. By the second act, however, even long-suffering Tom has had enough, and Spencer Tracy masterfully portrays his character's evolution from trusting husband to a man wracked with suspicion and ever-increasing rage.

At one point, tired of his wife's lies, Spencer's character has had enough and shouts, "Lies! All of it! Every word a lie! And another and another and another!" The emotion that Spencer fuses into the dialogue is palpable, and by the time he's through, the Becky character is shaking her head in silence. Even this is a provocation for the man Spencer plays, as he exclaims, "Don't shake your head! I know what I'm talking about and for the first time with you, I believe!"

The actress who played Becky would later admit that Spencer's performance was so powerful that night that she was "truly frightened" during part of his delivery. Actors are at their best when the emotions they convey are perceived as authentic, and Spencer Tracy's delivery was so raw and emotional that even his leading lady couldn't help but be affected by it. Soon after Spencer's powerful delivery, a review in the Rippon school paper congratulated him on his performance. The paper declared, "His steadiness, his reserve strength and suppressed emotion were a pleasant surprise to all who heard him as Tom Warder."

Around the same time, Spencer became involved with one of his fellow students—and a budding actress in her own right—Olive Foat, who was known by her middle name Lorraine. It's said that Ms. Foat was the only student at Rippon who was just as obsessed with acting as Spencer Tracy. The two kindred spirits would rehearse parts and discuss acting for hours on end, and in the fall of 1921, they both tried out for leading roles in a production of *The Great Divide*.

The pair had made a pact beforehand in which they determined that they would only act in the play if they both landed the parts they sought after. Lorraine managed to get accepted for the leading role of the female protagonist, Ruth Jordan, but the best Spencer could do was get accepted for a minor part as Ruth's sibling, Philip. Spencer wasn't going to settle for this bit part, and in a show of her solidarity with Spencer, Lorraine decided to drop out of the play as well.

Lorraine's rejection of a leading role caused quite a bit of talk on campus—so much so that the Dean took her to task for it. As Lorraine would later recall, "The Dean called me in to question my refusal and suggested that perhaps the reason Spence didn't get the part was because he had been neglecting his studies. That didn't satisfy me, although I knew that Spence wasn't too enthusiastic about studying. That was when we decided we'd have our own acting company with rehearsals at my house, and we called ourselves 'The Campus Players.'"

Yes, Spencer and Lorraine decided that if they could not get what they wanted from those who called the shots at Rippon's theater department, they would go into business for themselves. Soon thereafter, both Spencer and Lorraine landed leading roles in a production of *The Valiant* and appeared on stage together at the Municipal Auditorium that October. Spencer and Lorraine rehearsed their roles religiously until the parts were almost second nature.

In this piece, Spencer played the role of a condemned inmate named Joe, and Lorraine acted as his sister. An emotional dialogue ensued over the fate of Spencer's character and what his death might mean for the family. In the story, Spencer's character had decided it would be best to tell his sister that she had him mistaken for another man and that her actual brother Joe had perished as a war hero. He figured it would be better for his family to believe this was his fate rather than knowing the ignominy of having a relative condemned. The production was a success for both Spencer and his partner Lorraine.

There has been much speculation about just what Spencer and Lorraine's off-set relationship was like, but Lorraine herself has always insisted that they were just friends and acting buddies much more than anything else. As Lorraine herself would later put it, "He took me to a dance once in a while. We'd dance once, and he'd say, 'Let's go in the balcony,' and we'd go up there and sit and watch everybody else dance. He wouldn't dance. It was too much effort. And he'd say, 'Let's go down to the greasy spoon and get some food.' And I put up with that because I liked to be in the plays with him. But I didn't date him; I dated other people—boys who danced!"

Spencer Tracy may not have known how to dance, but he would soon prove to the world just how well he could act.

Chapter Two

Marriage and Children

"Acting is not the noblest profession in the world, but there are things lower than acting. Not many, mind you—but politicians give you something to look down on from time to time."

—Spencer Tracy

As Tracy's acting gigs picked up, he was able to get wider recognition by performing at the American Academy of Dramatic Arts in New York. It was on the strength of this performance that Tracy was awarded a scholarship to attend the academy.

Beginning his coursework in the spring of 1922, Tracy now put everything he had into his acting. He moved into a tiny New York apartment with a fellow student, where he tried to be as frugal as possible. Living on nothing but beans, rice, and his dreams of superstardom, Spencer Tracy gave it his all. He charged full speed ahead, with coursework that focused on everything from the refinement of his voice, his posture, his breathing, to even his own personal hygiene. Nothing was considered too insignificant when it came to the molding of actors at the academy.

Tracy made his New York debut on stage on October 20, 1922. On this date, he starred in a theatrical production of *The Wedding Guests*. The play was performed at the prestigious Carnegie Lyceum, and it was a major break for Spencer Tracy. He did well enough at the academy in the meantime, and by his senior year, he was touring with the academy's stock company, for which he performed in several plays every month.

It was these efforts that eventually led to a non-speaking part on Broadway as a robot in the Czech masterpiece "R.U.R." Tracy then finished up his schooling with the academy in the spring of 1923. Shortly after graduating from the academy, Tracy left for Cincinnati, Ohio, to try his luck there. When this came to nothing, he ended up back in New York.

Shortly after his return to the New York acting circuit, Tracy became involved with an actress by the name of Louise Treadwell. In a similar fashion to his previous relationship with Lorraine, Spencer and Louise initially hit it off due to their dedication to acting. The relationship soon became a little more than just professional, however, and by May, the couple was openly speaking of marriage. They would follow through with their plans and end up getting wed on September 10, 1923.

It was that very fall that Tracy managed to get a bit part on Broadway in a production called *A Royal Fandango*. Unfortunately, the production proved to be a complete bust, and after just 25 showings, it was pulled due to a lack of interest on the part of theatergoers. Although it most certainly wasn't because of the part he played in the production, Spencer Tracy couldn't help but take this rejection personally, and as he would later recall, his "ego took an awful beating."

More bad news awaited Spencer Tracy in January of 1924 when he joined an acting company in Winnipeg, only for it to shut down a short time later. His wife Louise had become pregnant in the meantime and would give birth to Spencer's first child—a baby boy named John—in June of 1924. Spencer was overjoyed to become a father, but that joy would turn to grief some twelve months later when it was realized that their son was deaf. Spencer's wife Louise had actually figured this out several months before but couldn't bring herself to tell her husband.

It's perhaps disturbing to contemplate, but Spencer Tracy—a bit of a superstitious man—came to believe that his son was born deaf as a "punishment for his sins." This sin was in reference to the fact that Spencer had been unfaithful while his wife was pregnant with his son. He had apparently had a fling with a woman named Betty Hanna. Spencer was convinced that his son was born deaf as a punishment for his indiscretion. Most people today would scoff at such beliefs, but Tracy apparently didn't believe in random coincidences and felt that he was somehow to blame for his son's inability to hear.

Sadly, it was this misguided belief that would lead Spencer to become estranged from both his son and his wife. In many ways, he began to bury himself in his work, and in the spring of 1926, he was knee-deep in his efforts with the acting troupe the Broadway Players. He received some moderate recognition that February, but audience turnout was in decline.

It wasn't until the following fall that Tracy was offered a break when he was given a leading role in a George M. Cohan piece entitled *Yellow*. Cohan was a renowned figure in the world of theater, and Spencer was excited about the role. In fact, he had declared to those close to him that if he didn't become a break-out star from this production, he was going to give up the acting world for good in favor of gaining employment "in a regular business instead." Spencer Tracy was hedging his bets, and it was now all or nothing.

Chapter Three

Struggling as an Actor

*"I couldn't be a director because I couldn't put
up with the actors. I don't have the patience.
Why, I'd probably kill the actors. Not to mention
some of the beautiful actresses."*

—Spencer Tracy

The Cohan theatrical production of *Yellow*
premiered on Broadway on September 21, 1926.
In this play, Spencer Tracy was cast in the role of
one Jimmy Wilkes, a newly married man who
does his best to mentor his best friend Chester
Morris, who can't seem to keep from getting into
trouble.

Although Spencer did the best that he could
with the part that he was given, the overall
production fell short. It wasn't exactly the smash
hit that Spencer Tracy had hoped for, and reviews
were mixed at best. Yet despite his declarations of
wanting to end his acting career if the results were
anything less than stellar, Spencer would continue

at his craft. George Cohan himself helped convince the actor to carry on, for despite the mixed reviews, Cohan knew a talented actor when he saw one, and he hoped to have Spencer on board for several more productions further down the road.

Spencer Tracy would later acknowledge just how much Cohan's feedback meant to him. He would later admit, "I'd have quit the stage completely if it hadn't been for George M. Cohan." Cohan could undoubtedly see a future in acting for Spencer, and he himself established part of it by writing Tracy into his next screenplay for *The Baby Cyclone.*

Once again, Tracy was cast in the role of a young, freshly married man, trying his best to figure out life. Unlike its predecessor, however, this play was a Broadway hit. If Spencer had given up after the more mediocre showing of *Yellow* as he had initially intended, he never would have seen the tremendous success that *The Baby Cyclone* would bring him.

During the course of the production of this play, Spencer became good friends with one of his fellow castmates—an actor named Grant Mitchell. Soon, he was having Grant over for dinner with his family. To the surprise of both

Spencer and Louise, Grant Mitchell seemed to hit it off well with their now toddler son, John. After getting acquainted with little John, Mitchel would then serve to enlighten Spencer and Louise with a new understanding in regard to John's condition.

Mitchell revealed that his own sister was deaf, and she had since grown up to be an intelligent and productive young woman. He even shared with them a recent letter, which bore testament to this fact. Baby John's mother Louise was particularly delighted. She would later recall, "He gave us her latest letter to read. Newsy, humorous, grammatically perfect, it obviously could not have been written by any other than an intelligent, well-educated, and altogether delightful person."

Again, it's perhaps hard for us to fathom today, but back then, parents often feared that their child would be doomed to an abnormal existence simply because they were hard of hearing. The testimony Grant Mitchell supplied the Tracys did indeed do wonders to alleviate their concerns.

At any rate, it was right on the heels of *The Baby Cyclone* that Spencer would star in another Cohan piece called *Whispering Friends*, which made its debut in 1928. It was a whimsical comedy number and probably a way to break up the monotony of the more intense roles Spencer had previously been cast in.

Sadly, while in the midst of this more light-hearted routine, Spencer Tracy would receive word that his father was on his deathbed. Spencer would later recall of his father's condition, "He got sick. And then he got sicker. Weak. And scared. He'd look at me beggingly—as though I could help if I wanted to. . . . Nothing to do but wait and suffer and wait and wait."

It is indeed a terrible thing to know that one of your loved ones is on an irreversible course of death, and all that's left to do is wait for that dreaded moment to arrive. Countless individuals whose family members are in hospice care—a treatment program designed not to cure illness but to merely ease the final symptoms—know all too well that sinking feeling of helplessness that Spencer Tracy describes.

Spencer, knowing that the show must go on, eventually got back on the stage, even while his father's condition worsened. After hearing that his father had finally passed, Tracy performed on stage as he normally did, hiding any sign of the emotional torment that he felt deep down inside. Shortly after his passing, Spencer Tracy, the dutiful son, was sure to attend the funeral mass held for his father at St. Mary's.

Immediately thereafter, Tracy was back on the road again to wrap up the rest of his scheduled appearances for *Whispering Friends*. It was once his whirlwind touring for *Whispering Friends* came to a close that Spencer came back to New York to be with his wife and son. Louise had since then had their son placed into a special school for deaf children called the Wright Oral School. Louise proved to be very much preoccupied with her son's schooling at the time, and Spencer, almost feeling like a third wheel, soon decided to leave home, stay out late, and hang out with friends instead.

Sometime during this break from acting, Tracy finally began to deal with the passing of his father. The sadness that he had so far controlled and somewhat suppressed soon came pouring out and was evidenced in a particularly touching letter that Tracy wrote to his mother during this time. The letter read in part, "I never let you know and never will again how much I miss my wonderful dad. I have come home at night and stood and cried before his picture in our front room." Tracy then continued in his remembrance of what his father meant to him, stating,

"Sometimes I want to go with him—I know I'd be alright where he is—and when that time comes, I'll hate to leave anyone behind, but I won't be afraid."

As touching as all this was, it must have been painfully concerning to Tracy's mother that her son was grieving so deeply. Tracy himself seemed to sense the somber, desolate tone of his words, and toward the end of the letter, he auto-corrected with, "But he is happy now and he is watching us and taking care of us, and he wants us to do our best and be happy—and we will. We have lots to live for."

Tracy pushed through his grief and was soon being offered new parts to play. As his experience and recognition continued to grow, he received another breakthrough role when he was cast in a production of *Dread*. The story is centered around a man in emotional anguish—a role that Tracy could quite obviously relate to considering his recent circumstances. The piece first premiered in the fall of 1929 with tremendous promise.

Dread was immediately overshadowed, however, by the events of October 29, 1929—for this was the day that the stock market crashed. This terrible financial disaster, which would send much of the world into the Great Depression, had an immediate effect on Tracy's acting career since the production of *Dread* had its finances severely curtailed in the fallout of the crash. In the aftermath, things would get so bad that Spencer's own mother would suggest that he leave the stage and get a regular job to support his family.

Things were indeed looking grim, but right when it looked like it was all over for his acting career, Spencer Tracy would hit the big time.

Chapter Four

Tracy's Breakthrough Moment

"It is up to us to give ourselves recognition. If we wait for it to come from others, we feel resentful when it doesn't, and when it does, we may well reject it."

—Spencer Tracy

In the aftermath of having his latest production pulled, Spencer Tracy found himself without work for three long, harrowing weeks. During this time, he seriously considered giving up acting, and his own mother encouraged him to do so. He would later claim that it was only the support of his wife Louise who kept him going. Despite their difficulties, Louise knew where Spencer's true passion was, and she did not want to see her husband abandon it.

It was tough, but Tracy hung in there and managed to snag a role in a play called *Veneer*.

He was actually a last-minute replacement for actor Henry Hull, who had initially been slated to play the leading man but had jumped ship in favor of taking a part in a comedy piece called *Michael and Mary*. Hull's loss was Tracy's gain, and Spencer was determined to make the best of it.

In this piece, Tracy gave a spirited portrayal of the main character, Charlie Riggs. It was enough to at least keep Spencer Tracy's name in circulation, and the recognition it provided paid off in the form of Tracy being recruited in January of 1930 for a lead part in *The Last Mile*. In this melodramatic piece, Spencer played the part of a convicted killer, waiting for his final sentence to be carried out.

Herman Shumlin, who produced the piece, was duly impressed with the way that Spencer Tracy handled the role. Shumlin was initially skeptical of Tracy, but it wasn't long before he began to sing his praises. As he would later describe it, "I was just about to dismiss him when something about our too-brief casting interview stayed with me. Since it was getting on to dinnertime, I invited him to join me at a theatrical haunt. There, in a less strained atmosphere, I was suddenly made aware as we were talking that, beneath the surface, here was a man of passion, violence, sensitivity and desperation: no ordinary man, and just the man for the part."

In *The Last Mile*, Tracy played a grim, condemned man not long for this world. It took a really special person to pull off such a character with authenticity. It was certainly no small feat, but Spencer Tracy did indeed manage to do it. Tracy performed the play on Broadway that spring and was so well received that he is said to have been given thunderous rounds of applause which endured long after the initial curtain call.

From beginning to end, the audience was fascinated by the play, which featured an all-male cast of convicts, who carried out their desperate dialogue to one another in recreated prison cells placed on center stage. Hearing Tracy and his comrades speaking of life and their looming death was quite stirring to theatergoers. Tracy, in his role as John 'Killer' Mears, in particular, stole the show with his honest and heartfelt delivery. He was praised in *TheNew York Times*, in which a critic roared, "Mears is a killer acted with muscular determination by Spencer Tracy."

After it was all said and done, Tracy was not only getting accolades for his performance but also much-needed cash flow. Since signing on for this production, he was getting $400 weekly, along with regular bonuses when box office returns merited it. Most importantly, as it pertained to his long-term prospects as an actor, his rave reviews got him the attention of the bigwigs in Hollywood.

Before long, Fox Studios came calling, which led to Spencer Tracy being cast for his film debut in *Up the River*. Staying in the same realm of gritty realism as *The Last Mile*, the film was initially supposed to be a grim drama. However, when MGM managed to release a prison drama that same year called *The Big House*, Fox opted to transform *Up the River* into more of a light-hearted, slapstick comedy. Producers were nervous about this change of course, but Tracy proved himself just as good with comedy sketch work as he was with dramatic dialogue and sequences.

In this film, Tracy plays the part of Saint Louis, a street-smart and hardened criminal who seeks to change his fortune. Tracy co-starred with Humphrey Bogart, who would become an undisputed legend in his own right. As it pertains to Tracy in particular, he was finally awarded a much-needed, long-term contract with a major motion picture company after signing on with Fox. Shortly thereafter, Spencer along with his wife and child were on their way to Hollywood, where Tracy would embark upon a long-lasting career in film.

Chapter Five

Hollywood Success

"Know your lines and don't bump into the furniture."

—Spencer Tracy

Upon getting settled into his new digs in California, Spencer Tracy started work on his next movie, *Quick Millions*. In this film, Tracy was once again cast as a hard-boiled and gruff character named Daniel J. "Bugs" Raymond. Released in 1931, the film stands in contrast with other crime films of the day such as *Little Caesar* and *The Public Enemy* by virtue of its less-lethal flavor. Rather than showing a steady stream of wanton violence, *Quick Millions* is content to wow audiences with dynamic dialogue rather than violent shootouts.

Tracy was by this point getting quite used to the role of miscreant and felt it was time for a change. That change came when he was cast in 1932's *Disorderly Conduct*. In this film, Spencer

Tracy plays the role of a policeman who gets tied up in the affairs of a prominent politician's daughter. The box office returns were fairly decent for this film, but it still wasn't a breakout success, and by the end of the year, Spencer Tracy had yet to become a household name. His family was growing in the meantime since it was that summer that his wife would give birth to their second child, a daughter named after her mother, Louise "Susie" Treadwell Tracy.

Rather than feeling closer to his family, Spencer Tracy was feeling increasingly isolated and continued to pour most of his time and energy into his work. Growing frustrated with the material that Fox was giving him to work with, Tracy considered not renewing his contract upon its expiration at the end of the year, but a sudden raise of $1,500 a week made him reconsider. However, despite the pay raise, the films he was cast for were a little less than promising. In 1932, he starred in pictures such as *Me and My Gal* and *20,000 Years in Sing Sing* with dismal results.

Spencer Tracy's real breakthrough role wouldn't arrive until *The Power and the Glory* in 1933. This movie employs a nice little flashback feature in which Tracy is portrayed as an older, successful man before flashing back to being a poor, young vagabond. Tracy followed up this piece by starring in *Shanghai Madness*, which had him play a leading romantic role. This film garnered much attention in regard to Tracy's magnetism as a leading man, but his next couple of movies would turn out to be flops.

Tracy became increasingly depressed at what seemed to be a failure to gain traction and is said to have turned to the bottle to drown his disappointment over his dismal box office returns. Things got so bad that by the summer of 1934 Tracy missed shooting while working on the movie *Marie Galante*. He had to be tracked down to a motel where he had passed out cold from a bout of binge drinking. This incident had serious ramifications for Spencer Tracy. The comatose Tracy was hauled off to an emergency room, and before he could even be revived, Fox ceased all payment to Spencer. Not only that, but he also had a lawsuit brought against him seeking some $125,000 in damages for interfering with the filming process.

Nevertheless, things would soon look up for Tracy when he entered into a new contract with MGM, just as the contract between Tracy and Fox fell apart. At this point, Spencer was more known for his antics off-set than he was for his actual performances on the silver screen. Still, executives at MGM were certain that they could mold Tracy into the kind of movie star they wanted him to be.

This theory was put to the test when Tracy was cast for the crime thriller *The Murder Man* in 1935. In this piece, Tracy starred alongside a young James Stewart, who was just then breaking out in the movies. Both Tracy and Stewart play the part of investigative reporters who specialize in murder cases. After *The Murder Man*, MGM switched up its tactics and began to place Tracy in a series of movies in which he was cast opposite of a female actress. In-demand actresses such as Jean Harlow and Myrna Loy were big box office draws and aided the returns of Tracy's films tremendously. Still, the star power of these women often seemed to reduce Tracy to more of a supportive role than the actual star of the movies.

In 1936, Tracy was finally able to prove that he could stand on his own when he starred in the film *Fury*. In this dramatic telling, Spencer plays the part of a man who, after nearly being killed by angry residents of a town, takes vengeance into his own hands. *Fury* managed to gain mostly positive reviews from audience-goers, and the box office returns weren't too shabby either, earning around 1.3 million dollars. Most importantly, this was the first real opportunity for Tracy to prove that he could become a major star without having to lean on the additional weight of a big-name co-star.

Nevertheless, his very next feature film, *San Francisco*, would have him back at sharing the limelight since here he would perform more of a supporting role for superstar Clark Gable. *San Francisco*, which is a musical disaster story based upon the 1906 San Francisco earthquake, had Tracy playing the part of a Catholic priest. This would probably not be a big deal for most actors, but for Spencer Tracer, who remained respectful (if not always faithful) of the Catholic faith throughout his life, it was important. Since Tracy viewed the office of the priesthood with such admiration and respect, he tried his best to portray both it and the Catholic Church in general in a good light. His reverence for the role apparently paid off because Tracy would receive an Oscar nomination for Best Actor thanks to his efforts.

San Francisco was a huge hit with moviegoers, who showed their appreciation with box office returns. In fact, it's said that this movie was the highest-grossing film that year. Tracy was rapidly climbing to the top, and thankful for his success, he pledged to put his alcohol-fueled days behind him. He informed his handlers at MGM that he was going to quit drinking, which further endeared him with the executives at the studio.

Now sober and with his head on straight, Tracy was able to finish up another smash hit called *Libeled Lady*. In this film, he shared the screen with popular starlet Jean Harlow as well as Myrna Loy and actor William Powell. Described as a "screwball comedy," this film does indeed have Tracy at his light-hearted best.

The truly goofball plot revolves around Myrna Loy's character Connie Allenbury. Connie has been subjected to a false story in the newspaper of having an affair and ends up suing the *New York Evening Star* as a result. Tracy plays the editor of the paper, who panics and concocts a hair-brained plot to have reporter Bill Chandler (played by Powell) get caught with Connie by his wife. The only problem is—he doesn't have a wife.

In order to correct this little detail of the plan, Tracy's character has Chandler marry his own fiancée Gladys Benton (played by Harlow). As one can imagine, Harlow's character is not too happy with the scheme, but in true comedic fashion, she ends up accepting her mission. The silly exchanges between characters were eagerly lapped up by movie-going audiences. Tracy now had yet another hit film before the year was out, proving that Tracy was now an established star in his own right.

Chapter Six

Academy Awards

"This mug of mine is as plain as a barn door.
Why should people pay 35 cents to look at it?"

—Spencer Tracy

The year 1937 was another good one for Spencer Tracy for it was that year that he managed to produce a string of hits, with films such as *Captains Courageous*, which earned him an Academy Award for Best Actor, as well as *Mannequin*, which had him share the screen with Joan Crawford. In *Mannequin*, Tracy shared much more than just the screen with Crawford since the two began to have a passionate off-set affair. Tracy had reconciled some of his family problems, but it was now more or less an open secret that he was routinely unfaithful to his wife, and his liaisons with Crawford were just the latest in a long history of infidelity.

Nevertheless, Tracy's career would continue to shine bright, and in 1938, he would break in the new year with another film with Clark Gable, called *Test Pilot*. In the film, Gable plays a courageous test pilot, willing to push the limits. Tracy plays the role of his friend, Gunner Morris. Tracy's character dies in one of the test flights at the end of the film, giving a sad but memorable final scene to Spencer Tracy as Gable's character tries to pull him free from the wreckage. The chemistry between Tracy and Gable was well known at this point, and this film served to even further establish them as a power duo in Hollywood.

Still, it was Tracy's next film—*Boys Town*—that would really generate recognition. In this movie, he was once again cast in the role of a man of the cloth, playing the priest Father Flanagan who founded the charity organization Boys Town. The movie was a tremendous success and the box office returns topped $4 million. It also netted Tracy another Academy Award for Best Actor. Tracy gave a memorable speech when he accepted the award, in which he stated in part, "I honestly do not feel that I can accept this award. I can accept it only as it was meant to be for a great man—Father Flanagan."

In other words, Tracy felt that the character he was playing was noble enough to deserve an award and that his mere portrayal of such a good man was not worthy of such praise. Then again, it was his ability as an actor, not being a good person for which the Best Actor award was handed out, so despite Tracy's claims to the contrary, it was indeed merited.

Tracy simply felt guilty about playing such a noble figure of high moral caliber when his own personal life was becoming increasingly troubled. He was taking part in frequent affairs and staying away from his family for long periods of time. At any rate, Spencer Tracy did indeed get his Oscar, but due to his remarks, a second was actually created and sent off to the real Father Flanagan, who was the inspiration behind the film.

After the success of *Boys Town*, Tracy took a short break before returning to the screen in 1939 with the film *Stanley and Livingstone*. This film is based on the real-life story of a reporter by the name of Sir Henry M. Stanley and his attempt to locate the famed explorer Dr. David Livingstone who had gone missing while on the continent of Africa. This film was produced by Fox, while Tracy was out on loan by MGM. To produce a successful film as an in-demand actor for the very company that had shunned him not so long ago was quite a reversal of fortune for Tracy.

Riding high on his success, in 1940, Tracy embarked upon a movie with stunning starlet Hedy Lamarr called *I Take This Woman*. It was a romantic piece, which had Tracy playing a psychiatrist who takes a suicidal woman played by Lamarr under his wing. The film was touted to be a masterpiece, but despite all the hype, the film ended up being a box office flop.

Nevertheless, Tracy persevered and managed to follow up this failure with a success by way of his work on the film *Northwest Passage*. This was a historical piece, and it made history for Tracy in particular since it was the first film he made in color, still a relatively new innovation in the 1940s. The film did well and was followed up by another fairly successful feature film, called *Edison, the Man*, in which Tracy played the part of the wily inventor Thomas Edison.

Tracy was praised for his performance, but the screenwriters at MGM were criticized for being too liberal with historical facts regarding Edison's life. In fact, a review in *TheNew York Times* declared, "When Metro deliberately distorts certain important details in Edison's career and boldly invents others . . . the question arises as to whether this creation is intended to be a reliable portrait of the great inventor or just another fellow who looks something like him. Frankly, we think it wiser to regard it in the second light." In other words, it was a good film, but in light of historical inaccuracies, it seemed more akin to a fictitious account of Edison's life than an honest retelling.

At any rate, Tracy was able to follow up this film with another smash hit by once again starring alongside Clark Gable for the movie *Boom Town*. Hedy Lamarr also appeared in this piece, and the star power coupled with good screenwriting was able to take the production over the top.

Doing well with MGM, Tracy quite eagerly renewed his contract when the time came in the spring of 1941. This new contract managed to promise $5,000 weekly while stipulating that Tracy would be unable to do more than three films per year. This was important since Tracy was beginning to feel a bit overworked and wanted to make sure that his efforts weren't taken lightly. He wasn't a machine after all; he had to have some time to himself away from sets and scripts. In the beginning, he had made himself as flexible as possible to get as much opportunity to act as he could, but now that he had made it to the top, he wouldn't have to overextend himself anymore. Instead of producers barking orders at

Tracy, it was now Spencer Tracy who would call the shots.

Chapter Seven

Tracy during World War II

"Love has nothing to do with what you are expecting to get—only with what you are expecting to give—which is everything."

—Katharine Hepburn

With a new contract in hand, 1941 promised to be a good year for Spencer Tracy. It was that year that he would go into the studio to film a sequel to his smash hit *Boys Town*. This film, which was to follow up the previous exploits of Father Flanigan, was called *Men of Boys Town*. The film featured a young Mickey Rooney and dealt with heavy concepts such as youths being mistreated at a juvenile detention facility.

This Father Flanigan film, just like its predecessor, had solid screenwriting, and Spencer Tracy and his fellow actors played their parts well. Their efforts were rewarded at the box office, and the film became one of the most successful showings of 1941. Closely following this film was a production of *Dr. Jekyll and Mr. Hyde* in which Tracy played Dr. Jekyll and his transformation into Mr. Hyde. He also starred alongside the famed Swedish actress Ingrid Bergman, with whom he would engage in a brief off-set affair.

The film itself was moderately successful, once again bringing in a profit at the box office. The reviews were fairly mixed, however, with some praising Tracy's performance, while others viewed his work as a little less than stellar. *TheNew York Times* carried a particularly harsh review, in which a critic proclaimed, "Mr. Tracy's portrait of Hyde is not so much evil incarnate as it is the ham rampant."

In 1942, Tracy was recruited to star alongside Katharine Hepburn in what would become an absolute classic, the film *Woman of the Year*. In this piece, Katharine Hepburn plays a journalist named Tess Harding, who is nominated for Woman of the Year for her work as a reporter. Tracy plays the part of Sam Craig, a sportswriter who falls in love with Hepburn's character. The film followed the light-hearted drama as the couple struggles to juggle love and career.

Woman of the Year depicts a man dedicated to his wife, but in reality, Spencer Tracy himself was not in a monogamous relationship. He and his wife Louise were still married and would remain so for the rest of their lives, but he was not faithful to his spouse. Katharine Hepburn would, in fact, become his latest fling, and the romance sparked between Tracy and Hepburn would continue over the next few decades.

This film was followed by a production of *Tortilla Flat*, which was based upon the John Steinbeck novel of the same name. The film did not do well, so MGM decided to return to what proved to be a money-making formula, recasting Spencer Tracy and Katharine Hepburn in yet another movie together. Rather than being a romantic comedy, their next pairing would be in a suspenseful thriller entitled *Keeper of the Flame*.

Although initial reviews were critical, the film ended up bringing in tremendous box office returns. The main criticism seems to stem from the fact that the characters and plot insinuate that wealth and money are equivalent to fascism while espousing left-leaning ideals that could almost be interpreted as communist in nature.

Tortilla Flat was followed by 1943's war-inspired *A Guy Named Joe*. This film, which seemed to magnify some of Tracy's best qualities as an actor, was an immediate success. It would end up being his biggest box office hit at this point in his career. After this film, Tracy would act in another war drama, *The Seventh Cross*, which would premiere in 1944. It was released at the height of World War II when the full horror of the Nazi occupation of Europe was just beginning to be understood. This film reflects this grim new understanding by depicting Tracy as an escaped prisoner fleeing from a concentration camp.

Close on the heels of this release was yet another war movie, this time depicting Tracy as an Allied pilot in *Thirty Seconds Over Tokyo*. After finishing up *Thirty Second Over Tokyo,* Tracy began to slow down so that he could better enjoy his newfound fame and fortune. In 1945, he would only star in one film, *Without Love*, in which he once again acted alongside Katharine Hepburn. At this point, their relationship had indeed become an open secret—just about everyone on set knew that Tracy and Hepburn were romantically involved, but MGM did what they could to keep the matter quiet.

After finishing up *Without Love,* Spencer decided to revisit theater by signing on for a play called *The Rugged Path*. Spencer was initially quite excited to get back into theater, telling the media, "I'm coming back to Broadway to see if I can still act." He would soon come to regret his return to Broadway, however, when his acting partnerships began to break down, and Tracy quite frankly became bored with the whole thing. Apparently, he began to get sick of following the rules of the director and having to repeat the same "lines over and over and over again every night." As if he was having an epiphany moment as to why he loved films so much, Tracy declared, "At least every day is a new day for me in films."

The following year though, Tracy wouldn't appear in a play or film. In 1946, Tracy would remain uncharacteristically quiet and inactive. It wouldn't be until the release of 1947's *The Sea of Grass* that the world would come to see Spencer Tracy once again. This was yet another Tracy/Hepburn film, which featured the couple in a western-styled drama. Critics were not too kind to this film, but despite initially negative reviews, fans loved it. Proving that movie-goers don't always go along with what critics might say, this film was a smash hit at the box office.

This success was followed up by another when Tracy starred alongside Lana Turner in the movie *Cass Timberlane*. This film did well, but many have noted that Lana Turner seemed to have simply outshined Tracy in this piece, and the critics took note.

Tracy then broke in 1948 by once again starring alongside Hepburn in a Frank Capra film called *State of the Union*. Tracy played a presidential candidate in the film; his character, Grant Matthews, is drafted into the race as the Republican nominee by his girlfriend Kay who is the driving force behind a newspaper influential with the Republican Party.

This film was timely since it was released in 1948 to coincide with the real-life election that would pit Democratic incumbent Harry Truman against Republican challenger Thomas E. Dewey. The Democrats were coming off a long run of holding the presidency. The former Democrat in office, Franklin D. Roosevelt, had been elected to serve an incredible four times (the first and only president to do so in U.S. history). He died in office during the fourth term, and Harry Truman, his vice president, had taken over.

The 1948 election would see Harry Truman running on his own merit, and many wondered if the unprecedented string of Democratic victories would finally be thwarted. In the film, Tracy's character was promoted as a possible alternative to Thomas Dewey. Despite the film's potentially partisan nature, it was generally well-received on both sides of the aisle.

Chapter Eight

Health Issues

"I'm tired of pretending that everything's fine just so I can please everyone else."

—Spencer Tracy

At the dawning of the 1950s, Spencer Tracy, now an older, veteran actor, was eager to show producers and audience-goers alike that he still had it. He wanted to show that he had what it took to make a blockbuster film, and when he finished up work on *Father of the Bride* in 1950, he managed to prove just that.

In this film, he plays the part of Stanley T. Banks. Mr. Banks is a man busy making preparations for his daughter's wedding. It's none other than an up-and-coming young Elizabeth Taylor who plays the blushing bride. Tracy fulfills the role of a well-meaning but sometimes bungling father in this romantic comedy. The film was well-received and earned some six million dollars in box office returns.

The film did so well, in fact, that the folks down at MGM thought it would be a good idea to do a sequel. Tracy was initially hesitant, afraid that he would ruin the goodwill he had generated with a shoddily done follow-up, but he needed not to worry. Tracy ultimately accepted the challenge, and in 1951, he and Elizabeth Taylor managed to craft a sequel called *Father's Little Dividend*, which proved to be very popular with movie-goers.

In 1952, Tracy was back to his partnership with Katharine Hepburn for the highly successful movie *Pat and Mike*. This piece had Hepburn playing a star athlete and Tracy reprising the role of a sports promoter. Whatever their roles were, Tracy and Hepburn always seemed to hit it off quite well with each other. Tracy's next film, however, was a tremendous flop. He took part in a history piece about Pilgrims, Puritans, and the Mayflower called *Plymouth Adventure*. No matter how well Tracy acted his part for this film, just about no one seemed interested in the subject matter. The film was also over-budgeted, and due to low box office returns, it resulted in a financial loss of almost two million dollars.

In 1954, MGM decided to loan Tracy out to Fox once again; this time, he took part in a western piece called *Broken Lance*. The film did well enough, and the movie itself would later win an Oscar for Best Story. The following year, in 1955, Tracy once again starred in a western, this time for *Bad Day at Black Rock*. This film would have Tracy himself nominated for an Academy Award for the Best Actor category.

Despite his good track record with MGM, by the time his contract was up for renewal, Tracy decided to go ahead and go solo, beginning work as a free agent in 1956. As an independent actor, Tracy once again appeared with Hepburn in 1957 for the feature film *Desk Set*. This was yet another romantic comedy, with all of the typical gags and light-hearted humor, but the movie-going public had finally gotten tired of this old formula that had worked so well in the past. The film didn't get much traction at the box office, and Tracy found himself becoming increasingly disillusioned.

The following year would see both a new direction and new success for Spencer Tracy, for it was this year that he would star in *The Old Man and the Sea*. The film was based on a novel by Ernest Hemingway, and Tracy seemed well poised for the part. There were early complaints though that Tracy had put on some weight and didn't quite fit the image Hemingway had in mind of his thin and gaunt protagonist. Despite these misgivings, and with the help of camera angling that hid some of Tracy's weight gain, Tracy was able to do an impressive job with the role and received yet another Oscar nomination.

Close on the heels of this piece, Tracy then starred in another political drama called *The Last Hurrah*. This film has Tracy playing the part of a mayor seeking re-election. While the movie received generally good reviews, the box office returns were rather dismal. For the first time in a long time, Tracy began to consider retiring from acting altogether. It seems that whenever Tracy felt backed in a corner with professional setbacks, he often considered quitting outright. Tracy would take another break from shooting and would not emerge until 1960, when he began work on *Inherit the Wind*.

Inherit the Wind was another historical piece, this time focusing on the famous Scopes Monkey Trial of 1925, in which schools argued over whether or not to have courses on evolution taught in the classroom. This piece would prove to be yet another film that would be received well by critics yet fail at the box office. Tracy's next film would fare better. Released in 1961, *The*

Devil at 4 O'Clock had Tracy once again cast in the role of priest. Adding to his own star power, he co-starred with Frank Sinatra in the movie, and the production was an overall success.

At this point in his life, however, Tracy began to be plagued by a slate of ever-increasing health problems. It wasn't until 1963 when Tracy was put in the hospital for what was described as a severe attack of breathlessness that his problems finally received a diagnosis. He was told that he had bad case of pulmonary edema. This was an often lethal condition in which the person's lungs would fill with fluid because the heart was failing to maintain proper, rhythmic beats. Along with this startling revelation was the news that Tracy had high blood pressure.

Tracy would slow down after this diagnosis, and not worrying too much about what anyone else might think, he opted to move in with Katherine Hepburn, who became a kind of full-time caregiver for her long-time lover. Tracy, unable to muster up the strength for a lead role, then settled for a smaller part in 1963's *It's a Mad, Mad, Mad, Mad World*. Despite his small role, this madcap comedy managed to become one of the big sellers of that year.

Tracy continued to struggle with his health meanwhile and ended up turning down two films, in both 1964 and 1965, respectively. In 1965, he was also given a further gloomy diagnosis, this time for hypertensive heart disease. In many ways, it seemed that Spencer Tracy's career was well behind him but little did anyone know, the best was still yet to come.

Chapter Nine

Late Life and Death

"A strange man, undoubtedly a great actor, but so wracked by personal problems."

—Fay Wray about Spencer Tracy

Struggling with health problems, Spencer Tracy did not return to the silver screen until he was cast in *Guess Who's Coming to Dinner* in 1967. This film was a ground-breaking piece which focused on an interracial couple. Tracy plays the part of a newspaper publisher whose daughter is engaged to a man of African American descent. The film had an all-star cast, with Katharine Hepburn as Tracy's on-screen wife and Hepburn's niece playing their onscreen daughter. The big-name star Sidney Poitier reprised the role of the daughter's fiancé.

The film was a thought-provoking piece at the time, yet it did well with audiences. To the surprise of many, the film even did well in the South where many Southerners typically frowned upon interracial marriage. The film won several Academy Award nominations, including Best Actor (for Spencer Tracy), Best Actress (for Katharine Hepburn), Best Film Editing, Best Story and Screenplay, and Best Picture.

Spencer Tracy would pay a high price for his hard work, however. Plagued with poor health throughout filming, he would end up dying just 17 days after the production wrapped up. It was in the early morning hours of June 10, 1967, that Tracy, who was staying with Katharine Hepburn at the time, got up from bed and went into the kitchen to pour himself some tea. Knowing that he was not feeling well, Hepburn got up and followed Tracy to the kitchen.

According to Hepburn, right when she was about to open the kitchen door, she heard a terrible crash and then the sound of Spencer falling to the floor. She rushed in to see her long-time lover crumpled on the ground, felled by a massive heart attack. Hepburn would later relate that although she was terribly sad about what had happened, she experienced a strange sensation. She had the unmistakable feeling that the 67-year-old actor Spencer Tracy, who had long been a troubled man, was finally at peace. As Hepburn later remarked, "He looked so happy to be done with living, which for all his accomplishments had been a frightful burden for him."

Spencer Tracy's work was over, and he was finally allowed to rest in peace.

Conclusion

Upon his passing, Tracy Spencer was given a proper Catholic funeral just as he would have wished. Mass was held for him on June 12 at Immaculate Heart of Mary Catholic Church, located in East Hollywood. Although Hepburn had long stood by Tracy, she agreed not to attend his funeral so as not to upset his wife and other family members.

Although she didn't attend, Hepburn played a key role in organizing Tracy's affairs. Many have long puzzled over it, but Louise and Katharine would remain on surprisingly good terms. It seems the two women had long ago accepted the fact that Tracy was dearly loved by them both. He was, of course, also dearly loved by his fans, and in the aftermath of his death, Spencer Tracy would be missed by all.

Bibliography

Curtis, James (2011). *Spencer Tracy: A Biography*.

Deschner, Donald (1972). *The Films of Spencer Tracy*.

Hepburn, Katharine (1991). *Me: Stories of My Life*.

Kanin, Garson (1971). *Tracy and Hepburn: An Intimate Memoir*.

New England Vintage Film Society Inc. (2012). *Spencer Tracy, a Life in Pictures: Rare, Candid, and Original Photos of the Hollywood Legend, His Family, and Career*.

Swindell, Larry (1969). *Spencer Tracy*.

Made in the USA
Monee, IL
15 October 2022

15938469R00036